ACOUSTIC ROCK

MELODY LINE, CHORDS AND LYRICS
FOR KEYBOARD • GUITAR • VOCAL

HAL•LEONARD®

ISBN-13: 978-1-4234-1338-7
ISBN-10: 1-4234-1338-5

HAL•LEONARD®
CORPORATION
7777 W. BLUEMOUND RD. P.O. BOX 13819 MILWAUKEE, WI 53213

Visit Hal Leonard Online at
www.halleonard.com

Welcome to the PAPERBACK SONGS® SERIES.

Do you play piano, guitar, electronic keyboard, sing or play any instrument for that matter? If so, this handy "pocket tune" book is for you.

The concise, one-line music notation consists of:

MELODY, LYRICS & CHORD SYMBOLS

Whether strumming the chords on guitar, "faking" an arrangement on piano/keyboard or singing the lyrics, these fake book style arrangements can be enjoyed at any experience level – hobbyist to professional.

The musical skills necessary to successfully use this book are minimal. If you play guitar and need some help with chords, a basic chord chart is included at the back of the book.

While playing and singing is the first thing that comes to mind when using this book, it can also serve as a compact, comprehensive reference guide.

However you choose to use this PAPERBACK SONGS® SERIES book, by all means have fun!

CONTENTS

ABOUT A GIRL

Words and Music by
KURT COBAIN

you hang me out to dry, ___ but

To Coda ⊕

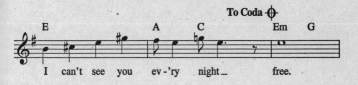

I can't see you ev -'ry night ___ free.

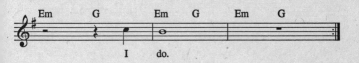

I do.

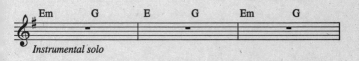

Instrumental solo

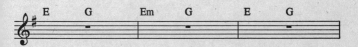

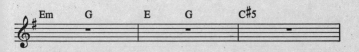

8

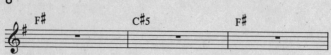

F#   C#5   F#

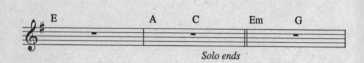

E   A   C   Em   G

Solo ends

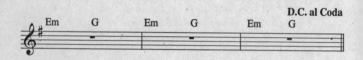

D.C. al Coda

Em   G   Em   G   Em   G

CODA

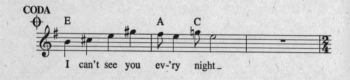

E   A   C

I can't see you ev-'ry night

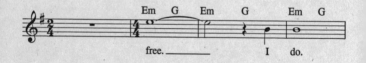

Em   G   Em   G   Em   G

free. _____   I   do.

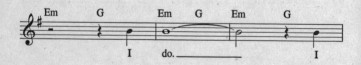

Em   G   Em   G   Em   G

I   do. _____   I

Em   G   Em   G   E5

do. _____   I   do.

ACROSS THE UNIVERSE

**Words and Music by JOHN LENNON
and PAUL McCARTNEY**

Slowly, and smoothly

Words are flow-ing out__ like end-less rain __ in-to a pa-per cup,__ they slith-er while__ they pass, they slip a-way __ A-cross The U-ni-verse. __

Pools of sor-row, waves of joy are drift-ing through my o-pened mind,__ pos-sess-ing and ca-ress-ing me.__

Jai __ Gu-ru__ De - va.__ Om.__

Noth-ing's gon-na change my world,__

Noth-ing's gon-na change my world.__

AMERICAN PIE

Words and Music by
DON McLEAN

Moderately

So bye - bye, Miss A - mer - i - can Pie_ drove my

Chev - y to the lev - ee but the lev - ee was dry._ Them

good ol' boys_ were drink - in' whis - key and rye_ sing - in'

this - 'll be the day_ that I___ die,

this - 'll be the day_ that I___ die.____

Did you _ write the book of love and do you_

have faith in God a-bove?_ If the Bi-ble tells_

you so_ now do you_ be-lieve_ in

rock and roll,_ can mu-sic save your mor-tal soul_ and

can you teach me how to dance_ real slow?_

_ Well, I know that you're in

love with him_ 'cause I_ saw you danc-in'

in the gym,_ you both kicked off_ your shoes._

14

Man I dig those rhy-thm and blues. _____ I was a lone-ly teen-age _ bronc-in' buck _ with a pink car-na-tion and a pick-up truck. _ But I knew I _ was out _ _____ of luck _ the day _ the mu- -sic died. _

D.S. al Coda

I start-ed sing-in'

CODA

this-'ll be the day _ that I _ die. _

BABY, I LOVE YOUR WAY ¹⁵

Words and Music by
PETER FRAMPTON

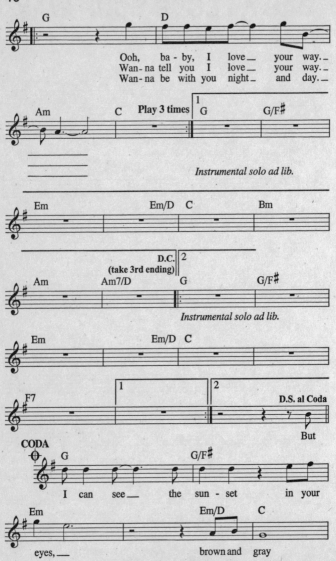

Ooh, ba - by, I love ___ your way. ___
Wan - na tell you I love ___ your way. ___
Wan - na be with you night ___ and day. ___

Play 3 times

Instrumental solo ad lib.

D.C.
(take 3rd ending)

Instrumental solo ad lib.

D.S. al Coda

But

CODA

I can see ___ the sun - set in your

eyes, ___ brown and gray

AMERICAN TUNE

Words and Music by
PAUL SIMON

Man - y's the time I've been mis - tak -
soul who's not been bat -

- en and man - y times con - fused.
tered, I don't have a friend who feels at ease.

Yes, and I've of - ten felt for - sak -
I don't know a dream that's not been shat -

- en and cer - tain - ly mis - used.
tered or driv - en to its knees.

Oh, but I'm al - right, I'm
Oh, but it's al - right, it's

al - right, I'm just wea - ry to my bones,
al - right, for we lived so well so long,

Am C F C G C
— We come in the ag - e's most un - cer -
G C Bdim Am E
- tain _ hours and sing an A - mer - i - can tune. ___
Am C9 F G
— Oh, _ and it's al - right, it's
F C G C F C G
al - right, it's al - right. _ You can't be for - ev - er blessed. _
Am A7 D7 G
— Still, to - mor - row's goin' _ to be an -
C G D G C
oth - er work - ing day, And I'm
F C G E Am Dm
try - ing to get _ some rest, _ That's all I'm
C/G G C F C
try - ing to get some rest.
G F C G C

ANGIE

Words and Music by MICK JAGGER
and KEITH RICHARDS

An-gie, An-gie, when will those clouds all dis-ap-pear?

An-gie,

An-gie, where will it lead us from

here? With no lov-ing in our souls and no

mon-ey in our coats, you can't say we're sat-is-fied,

but An-gie, An-gie,

you can't say we nev-er tried.

An - gie, ___ you're beau-ti-ful,

but ain't it time we said good-bye? _____

An - gie, I still love _ you,

re-mem-ber all _ those nights we cried? _____ All the

dreams we held _ so close _ seemed to all _ go up in smoke, _

let me whis - per in your ear; _____

"An-gie, An-gie, where will it lead us from

here?" ____ (Instrumental)

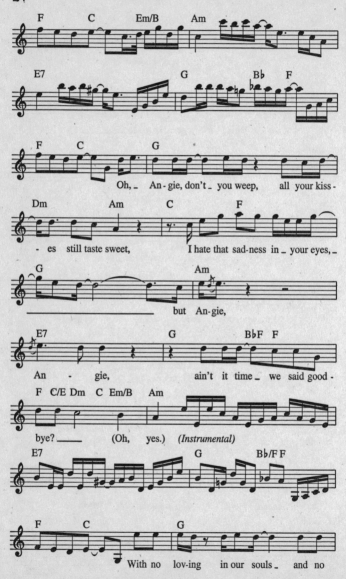

Oh, __ An-gie, don't __ you weep, all your kiss-es still taste sweet, I hate that sad-ness in __ your eyes, __ but An-gie,

An - gie, ain't it time __ we said good-bye? ____ (Oh, yes.) *(Instrumental)*

With no lov-ing in our souls __ and no

BABE, I'M GONNA LEAVE YOU

Words and Music by ANNE BREDON,
JIMMY PAGE and ROBERT PLANT

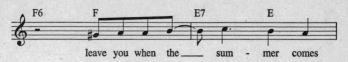

leave you when the___ sum - mer comes

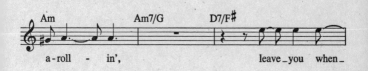

a - roll - in', leave _ you when _

___ the sum - mer _ comes _ a - long. _

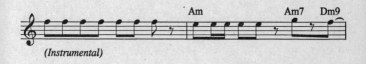

(Instrumental)

Babe, babe, _ babe, ___ babe, _ babe, _

_ babe, _ ba - by, mm, ba - by I ___

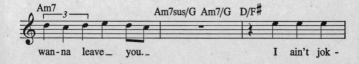

wan - na leave _ you. _ I ain't jok -

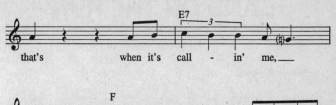

that's   when it's   call - in'   me, ___

I   said that's when it's

call - in'   me ___   back _ home. ___

Additional Lyrics

I've got to quit you, yeah. Oh, baby, baby, baby, baby
Baby, baby, baby, oh don't you hear it callin' me?
Oh, woman, woman, I know, I know. Feels good to have you back again
And I know that one day baby, it's gonna really grow, yes it is.

We gonna go walkin' through the park every day.
Oh, my babe, ev'ry day. Oh my, my, my, my, my, my, babe. I'm gonna leave you
Go away. Oh, huh. So good, sweet baby. It was really, really good.
You made me happy ev'ry single day, but now I've got to go away. Oh, oh, oh.

BAND ON THE RUN

Words and Music by
PAUL and LINDA McCARTNEY

Moderately bright

1. Well, the rain ex-plod - ed with a
un - der-tak - er drew a
3. *(See additional lyrics)*

might - y crash_ as we fell in - to_ the sun,_
heav - y sigh_ see - ing no one else_ had come,_

and the first one said to the
and a bell was ring-ing in the

sec - ond one there_ I hope you're hav - ing fun._
vil - lage square_ for the rab - bits on the run._

Band on the run,_

band on the run;_ and the

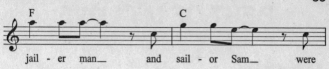

jail - er man___ and sail - or Sam___ were

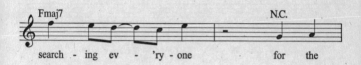

search - ing ev - 'ry - one for the

band on___ the run,___ band on___ the run,___

___ band on___ the run,___

band on___ the run.___ 2. Well, the

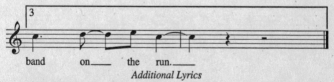

band on___ the run.___

Additional Lyrics

3. Well, the night was falling as the desert world began to settle down.
In the town they're searching for us ev'rywhere but we never will be found.
Band on the run; band on the run;
And the country judge who held a grudge will search for evermore.
For the band on the run, band on the run,
Band on the run, band on the run.

BEST OF MY LOVE

Words and Music by JOHN DAVID SOUTHER,
DON HENLEY and GLENN FREY

BLACKBIRD

**Words and Music by JOHN LENNON
and PAUL McCARTNEY**

Slowly and smoothly

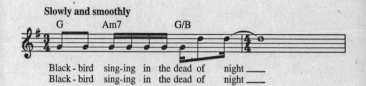

Black - bird sing-ing in the dead of night ____
Black - bird sing-ing in the dead of night ____

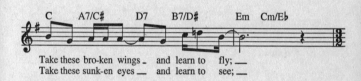

Take these bro-ken wings _ and learn to fly; ____
Take these sunk-en eyes _ and learn to see; ____

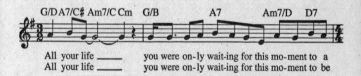

All your life ____ you were on-ly wait-ing for this mo-ment to a
All your life ____ you were on-ly wait-ing for this mo-ment to be

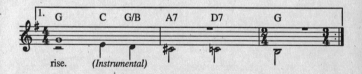

1.
rise. (Instrumental)

2.
free. Black - bird, ____ fly, ____

Black - bird, __ fly, _____ in - to the

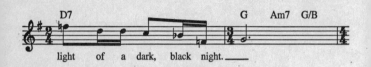

light of a dark, black night. ___

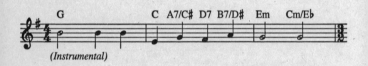

(Instrumental)

Black - bird, _ fly, __ Black - bird, _ fly, _

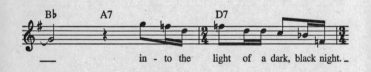

_ in - to the light of a dark, black night. _

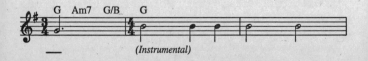

_ *(Instrumental)*

CHANGE THE WORLD

**Words and Music by WAYNE KIRKPATRICK,
GORDON KENNEDY and TOMMY SIMS**

42

COME TO MY WINDOW

Words and Music by
MELISSA ETHERIDGE

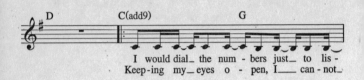

I would dial_ the num - bers just_ to lis -
Keep-ing my_ eyes o - pen, I_ can - not_

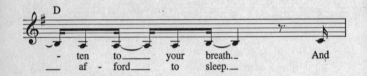

\- ten to_ your breath._ And
_ af - ford_ to sleep._

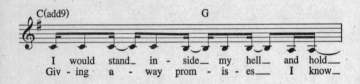

I would stand_ in - side_ my hell_ and hold_
Giv - ing a - way prom - is - es_ I know_

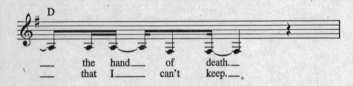

_ the hand_ of death._
_ that I_ can't keep._

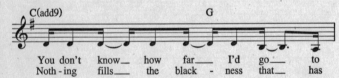

You don't know_ how far_ I'd go_ to
Noth - ing fills_ the black - ness that_ has

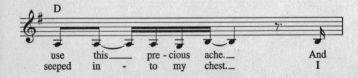

use this_ pre - cious ache._ And
seeped in - to my chest._ I

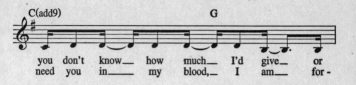

you don't know___ how much___ I'd give___ or
need you in___ my blood,___ I am___ for -

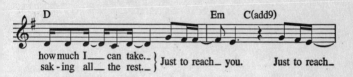

how much I___ can take..
sak-ing all___ the rest.__ } Just to reach__ you.   Just to reach___

— you.___ Oh, to___ reach__ you,_____

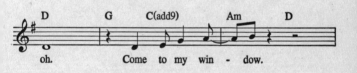

oh.   Come   to my win - dow.

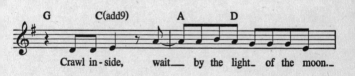

Crawl in - side,   wait___ by the light__ of the moon.__

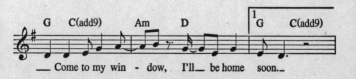

— Come to my win - dow, I'll__ be home   soon.__

soon._

I don't care ___ what ___ they think._

I don't care ___ what ___ they say. ___

What do they know a - bout this _ love _

an - y - way? ___

___ Come, _

___ come _ to my _ win - dow, I'll _ be home, _ I'll _

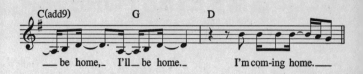

_ be home,_ I'll_ be home._ I'm com-ing home._

Come to my win - dow,

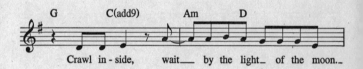

Crawl in - side, wait_ by the light_ of the moon._

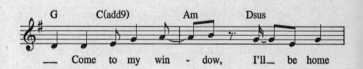

_ Come to my win - dow, I'll_ be home

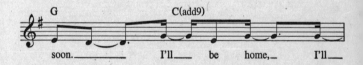

soon._____ I'll_ be home,_ I'll

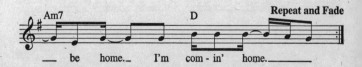

_ be home._ I'm com - in' home._

48

CLOSE MY EYES FOREVER

Words and Music by LITA FORD
and OZZY OSBOURNE

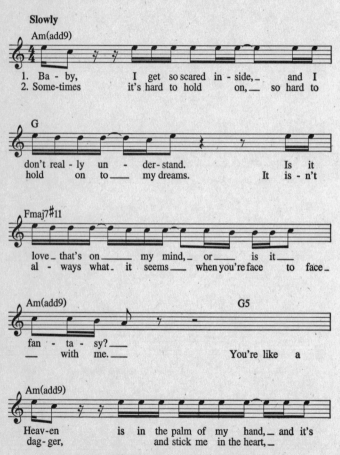

Will you ev - er take _ me?

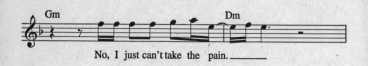

No, I just can't take the pain. _____

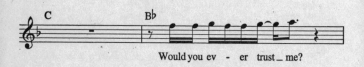

Would you ev - er trust _ me?

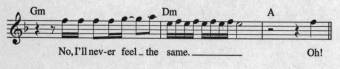

No, I'll nev-er feel _ the same. _____   Oh!

(Instrumental)

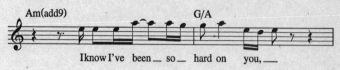

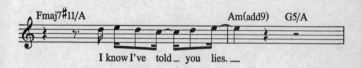

I know I've been — so — hard on you, —

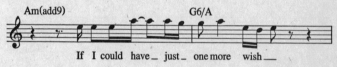

I know I've told — you lies. —

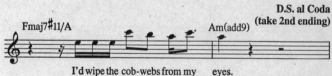

If I could have — just — one more wish —

D.S. al Coda
(take 2nd ending)

I'd wipe the cob-webs from my eyes.

CODA

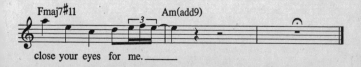

Close your eyes.   Close your eyes.   You got-ta

close your eyes for me. _____

CRAZY LITTLE THING CALLED LOVE

Words and Music by
FREDDIE MERCURY

54

(Instrumental)

I got - ta be cool

re - lax, _ get hip, _ get

on my tracks, _ take a back seat, hitch - hike, _ And

take a long ride on my mot - or - bike _ un - til I'm

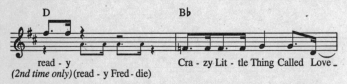

read - y   Cra - zy Lit - tle Thing Called Love _
(2nd time only) (read - y Fred - die)

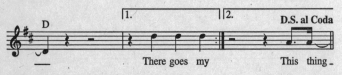

1.   2.   D.S. al Coda

_ There goes my   This thing _

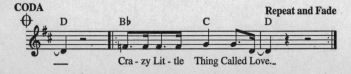

CODA   Repeat and Fade

_ Cra - zy Lit - tle Thing Called Love. _

FAST CAR

Words and Music by
TRACY CHAPMAN

Moderately

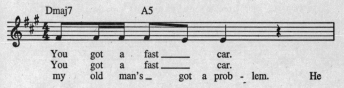

You got a fast ____ car.
You got a fast ____ car.
my old man's ____ got a prob - lem. He

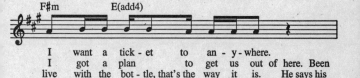

I want a tick - et to an - y - where.
I got a plan to get us out of here. Been
live with the bot - tle, that's the way it is. He says his

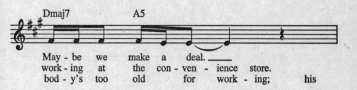

May - be we make a deal. ____
work - ing at the con - ven - ience store.
bod - y's too old for work - ing; his

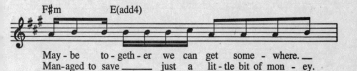

May - be to - geth - er we can get some - where. ____
Man - aged to save ____ just a lit - tle bit of mon - ey.
bod - y's too young ____ to look like his. My

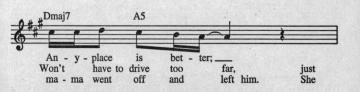

An - y - place is bet - ter; ____
Won't have to drive too far, just
ma - ma went off and left him. She

start - ing from ze - ro, got noth - ing to lose.
'cross the bor - der and in - to the cit - y.
want - ed more from life __ than he could __ give. I said

May - be we'll make some - thing.
You and I can both get jobs and
some - bod - y's got to take care of him, so

Me my - self, I've got noth - ing to prove.
fi - n'lly see __ what it means to be liv - ing.
I quit school and that's what I did.

(Instrumental)

1,2

3

(3.) See

You got a fast __ car. Is it

fast e - nough __ so we could fly a - way? __

We got - ta make a de - cis - ion;

F#m / **E(add4)**

leave to - night __ or live and die this way.

Dmaj7 / **A5** / **F#m** / **E(add4)**

(Instrumental)

Dmaj7 / **A5**

I re - mem - ber when we were

D

driv - ing, driv - ing in your car, __

A

speed so fast __ I felt like __ I was drunk.

F#m

cit - y lights lay out be - fore __ us and your

Esus / **D** / **F#m**

arms felt nice wrapped 'round my shoul - der. And I _____ had a

E / **D** / **F#m**

feel - ing that I __ be - longed. __ I _____ had a

58

CRAZY ON YOU

Words and Music by ANN WILSON, NANCY WILSON and ROGER FISHER

Moderately fast Rock

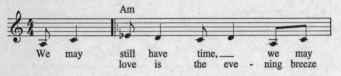

We may still have time, ___ we may
love is the eve - ning breeze

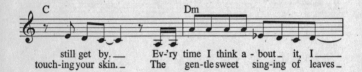

still get by. ___ Ev - 'ry time I think a - bout __ it, I ___
touch-ing your skin. __ The gen - tle sweet sing - ing of leaves __

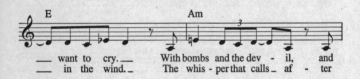

__ want to cry. __ With bombs and the dev - il, and
__ in the wind. __ The whis - per that calls __ af - ter

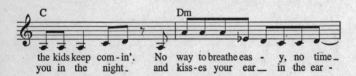

the kids keep com - in'. No way to breathe eas - y, no time __
you in the night __ and kiss - es your ear __ in the ear -

__ to be young. _____
ly __ light. _____

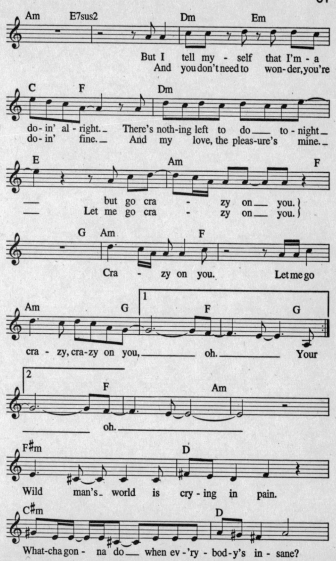

DUST IN THE WIND

Words and Music by
KERRY LIVGREN

EVERY ROSE HAS ITS THORN

Words and Music by BOBBY DALL, BRETT MICHAELS, BRUCE JOHANNESSON and RIKKI ROCKETT

68

FREE FALLIN'

Words and Music by TOM PETTY
and JEFF LYNNE

Moderate Rock

She's a good girl; _ loves her ma - ma, loves

Je - sus, _ and A - mer - i - ca too. _ She's a

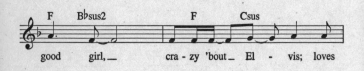

good girl, _ cra - zy 'bout _ El - vis; loves

hors - es _ and her boy-friend too. _

It's a

72

fall - in'.   All the

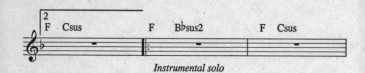

Instrumental solo

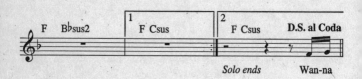

Solo ends   Wan-na

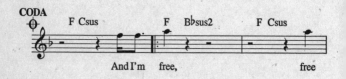

And I'm   free,   free

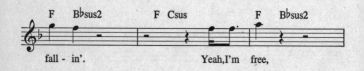

fall - in'.   Yeah, I'm free,

free   fall - in'.   And I'm

GIVE A LITTLE BIT

Words and Music by RICK DAVIES
and ROGER HODGSON

Moderately slow Rock Ballad

Give a lit - tle bit, _____

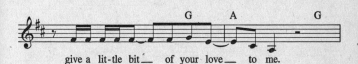

give a lit-tle bit __ of your love __ to me.

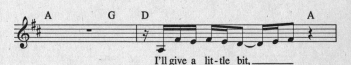

I'll give a lit - tle bit, _____

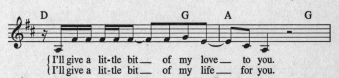

{ I'll give a lit-tle bit __ of my love __ to you.
I'll give a lit-tle bit __ of my life __ for you.

There's so much __ that we need __
Now's the time __ that we need __

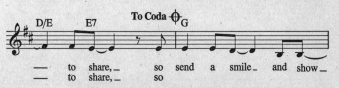

— to share, __ so send a smile __ and show __
— to share, __ so

— sur-prised. —

Instrumental solo ad lib.

Aah. —

find your-self, — we're on — our way — back home. —

— Oh, go-in' home. —

Don't you need, don't you need to feel — at home. —

— Oh, yeah, — we got-ta sing. —

HELP ME MAKE IT THROUGH THE NIGHT

Words and Music by
KRIS KRISTOFFERSON

Take the rib - bon from your hair,
Come and lay down by my side
Yes - ter - day is dead and gone

Shake it loose and let it
Till the ear - ly morn - in'
And to - mor - row's out of

fall, _____
light. _____
sight, _____

Lay - in'
All I'm
And it's

soft up - on my skin. _____
tak - in' is your time. _____
sad to be a - lone. _____

1.
Like the shad - ows on the wall.

2.
(To next strain)
Help Me Make It Through The Night.

HELPLESSLY HOPING

Words and Music by
STEPHEN STILLS

hear   a good - bye, _____ or
say- in' she is lost _____ and

e - ven _____ hel - lo? _____
chok - ing _____ on hel - lo. ___

_____ } They are

one _____ per - son, they are two_

_ a - lone, _____ they are three_

_ to - geth - er, they are for_

_____ each oth - er.

I'D LOVE TO CHANGE THE WORLD

Words and Music by
ALVIN LEE

Bright Folk Rock

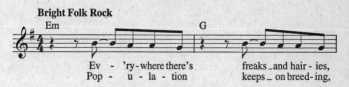

Ev - 'ry-where there's freaks and hair - ies,
Pop - u - la - tion keeps on breed-ing,

dykes and fair - ies. Tell me, where is
na - tion bleed-ing, still more feed-ing

san - i - ty?
e - con - o - my.

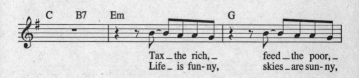

Tax the rich, feed the poor,
Life is fun - ny, skies are sun - ny,

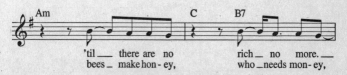

'til there are no rich no more.
bees make hon - ey, who needs mon - ey,

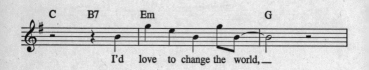

mo-nop - o - ly? —

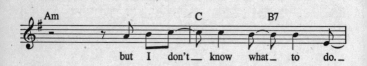

I'd love to change the world, —

but I don't — know what — to do. —

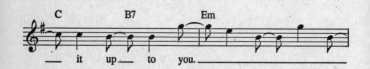

— So I'll leave —

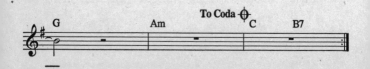

— it up — to you. —

To Coda

—

Guitar solo

World – pol-lu - tion, there's no so-lu - tion,

in - sti -tu - tion, e-lec - tro-cu - tion.

Just black or white, _ rich or poor, _

them and us, _ stop the war. _

D.S. al Coda

CODA

solo ends

(2.) I'd

IRIS

Words and Music by
JOHN RZEZNIK

With a steady pulse

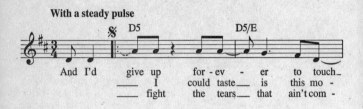

And I'd give up for-ev-er to touch
___ I could taste ___ is this mo-
___ fight the tears ___ that ain't com-

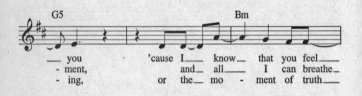

___ you 'cause I ___ know ___ that you feel ___
- ment, and all ___ I can breathe ___
- ing, or the ___ mo- ment of truth ___

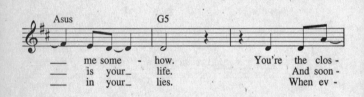

___ me some - how. You're the clos-
___ is your ___ life. And soon-
___ in your ___ lies. When ev-

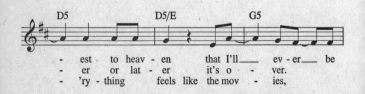

- est to heav- en that I'll ___ ev- er be
- er or lat- er it's o - ver.
- 'ry - thing feels like the mov - ies,

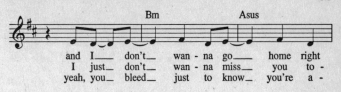

and I___ don't___ wan - na go___ home right
I just___ don't___ wan - na miss___ you to -
yeah, you___ bleed___ just to know___ you're a -

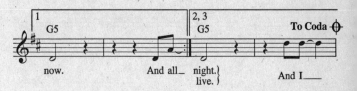

now.   And all___ night.
              live.

And I___

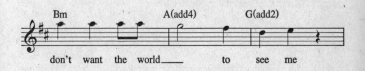

don't want the world___   to   see   me

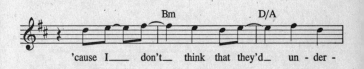

'cause I___ don't___ think that they'd___ un - der -

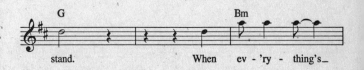

stand.   When   ev - 'ry - thing's___

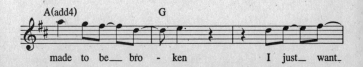

made to be___ bro - ken   I just___ want___

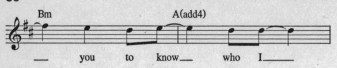

Bm   A(add4)

___ you to know___ who I___

G   Bm   Bm9

am.   *(Instrumental)*

Gmaj7   Bm   Bm9

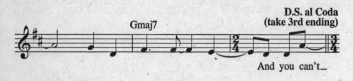

D.S. al Coda
(take 3rd ending)

Gmaj7

And you can't___

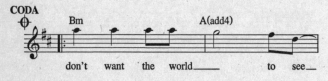

CODA

Bm   A(add4)

don't want the world___ to see___

G(add2)   Bm

___ me   'cause I___ don't___ think that they'd___

D/A   G

___ un - der - stand.   When

ev - 'ry - thing's— made to be— bro - ken

I just— want— you to know— who I—

1
am._____ And I—

2
am._ I just— want— you to know—

— who I— am. I just— want—

1, 2

3
am._____ *Instrumental solo*
(Vocal 1st time only)

Repeat and Fade

LANDSLIDE

Words and Music by
STEVIE NICKS

fraid of__ chang - ing   'cause I

built   my__ life_____ a - round_ you. __

But   time_____ makes_ you   bold - er.

Chil - dren_ get   old - er__ and I'm____ get ting old -

- er,   too.   So...__

(Instrumental)

LAYLA

**Words and Music by ERIC CLAPTON
and JIM GORDON**

Moderately slow Shuffle ♩. = 92

1. What will you do when you get lone - ly? ___

No ___ one wait-ing by your ___ side. ___

You've ___ been run - nin', ___ hid-in' much too long. ___

You know it's just your fool-ish pride. ___ Lay - la, ___

___ got me on my knees. Lay - la, ___

___ beg - gin' dar - lin', please. Lay - la, ___

___ dar - lin' won't you ease my wor - ried

Dm **Bb** **C** **N.C.** **A** **C**

mind? __

C#m7 **G#7**

2. Tried to give you con-sol-a - tion, __
3. Make the best of the sit - u - a - tion, __

C#m7 **C** **D** **E** **E7**

your old man had let you down. __
before I fin - ally go in - sane. __

F#m **B** **E** **A**

Like __ a __ fool, I fall in love with you.
Please __ don't __ say we'll nev-er find a way.

F#m **A** **E** **A**

You turned my whole world up-side down.)
Tell me all my love's in vain.) Lay - la, __

Dm **Bb** **C** **Dm**

__ got me on my knees. Lay - la, __

Bb **C** **D5** **Dm**

__ beg - gin' dar - lin', please. __ Lay - la, __

Bb **C** **D5** **Dm**

__ dar - lin', won't you ease my wor - ried

1.
Bb **C** **A** **C**

mind? __

2.
Bb **C**

mind? __

LEADER OF THE BAND

Words and Music by
DAN FOGELBERG

Gently

An on - ly child a - lone and wild a
A qui - et man of mu - sic de -

cab - 'net mak - er's son,
nied a sim - pler fate,

his hands were meant for dif - f'rent work and his
He tried to be a sol - dier once but his

heart was known to none.
mu - sic would - n't wait.

He left his home and went his lone and
He earned his love through dis - ci - pline a

sol - i - tar - y way and he
thun - d'ring vel - vet hand His

gave to me___ a gift___ I___ know___ I
gen - tle means___ of sculpt - ing___ souls___ took

nev - er can re - pay. *(Instrumental)*
years to un - der -

stand.

The lead - er of the band___ is tired___ and___ his

eyes are grow - ing old.___ But his

blood runs through my___ in - stru - ment___ and his

song is in my soul._____

My life has been a poor___ at - tempt___

to im-i-tate the man, ___ I'm just a liv-ing leg-

- a-cy ___ to the lead-er of ___ the band. *(Instrumental)*

My broth-ers' lives were dif - f'rent ___ for they
I thank you for the mu - sic ___ and your

heard an-oth-er call. ___ One went to Chi-ca-
sto - ries of the road, ___ I thank you for the free -

- go ___ and the oth - er to St. Paul. ___
- dom when it came my time to go. ___

And I'm in Col - o - ra - do ___ when I'm
I thank you for the kind - ness ___ and the

not in some ___ ho - tel ___
times when you ___ got tough ___ and

99

in - stru - ment___ and his song is in my
soul.___ My life has been a poor___
___ at - tempt___ to im - i - tate the man,___
___ I'm just a liv - ing leg -
- a - cy___ to the lead - er of___ the band.___ I
am the liv - ing___ leg - a - cy___ to the
lead - er___ of___ the band.___

(Instrumental)

LEAVING ON A JET PLANE

Words and Music by
JOHN DENVER

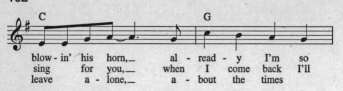

blow - in' his horn,___ al - read - y I'm so
sing for you,___ when I come back I'll
leave a - lone,___ a - bout the times

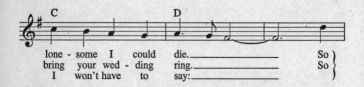

lone - some I could die._____ So
bring your wed - ding ring._____ So
I won't have to say:_____ So

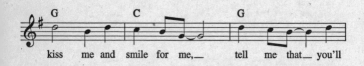

kiss me and smile for me,___ tell me that___ you'll

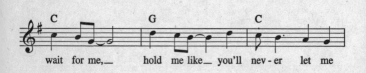

wait for me,___ hold me like___ you'll nev - er let me

go._____ 'Cause I'm leav - in'

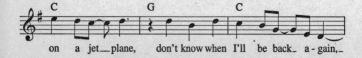

on a jet___ plane, don't know when I'll be back___ a - gain,___

LOVE OF A LIFETIME

Words and Music by BILL LEVERTY
and CARL SNARE

Slow Rock Ballad

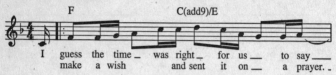

I guess the time _ was right _ for us _ to say _
make a wish and sent it on _ a prayer. _

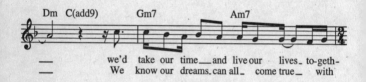

_ we'd take our time _ and live our lives _ to-geth
_ We know our dreams can all _ come true _ with

- er day _ by _ day. _ We'll
love that we _ can share. _ With

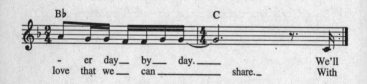

you I nev - er won - der,

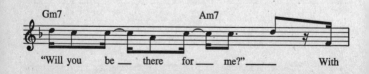

"Will you be _ there for _ me?" _ With

106

ev - er in my heart. _____ I

fi - n'lly found _ the Love _____ Of A Life -

- time. ___ With

ev - 'ry kiss, _ our love _ is like _ brand new _

_ and ev-'ry star _ up in _ the sky _ was made _

_ for me ___ and you. ___

Still, we both _ know that _ the road _ is long, _ but we

Gm7 Am7
know that we will be to - geth - er be -
B♭ C D.S. al Coda
cause our love is strong. I
CODA
F C/E Dm C B♭ F/A
- time.
Gm7 C
Oo, I
G Bm7
fi - n'lly found the Love Of A Life -
C D/F♯
- time, a
G Bm7
love to last my whole life through.

MAGGIE MAY

Words and Music by ROD STEWART
and MARTIN QUITTENTON

Medium Rock beat

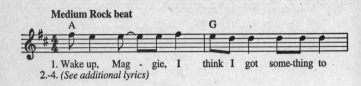

1. Wake up, Mag - gie, I   think I got some-thing to
2.-4. *(See additional lyrics)*

say   to   you. ___   It's

late Sep - tem - ber and I   real - ly should ___ be   back ___

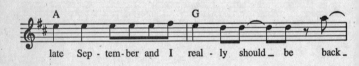

___ at ___ school. ___   I

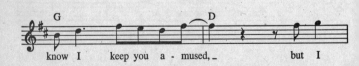

know I   keep you a - mused, ___   but I

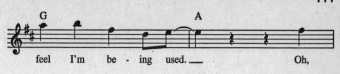

111

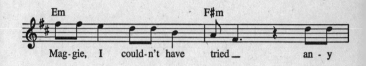

feel I'm be - ing used. ___ Oh,

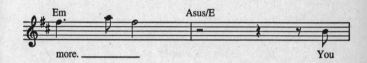

Mag - gie, I could-n't have tried ___ an - y

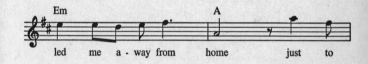

more. _____ You

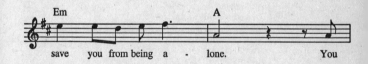

led me a - way from home just to

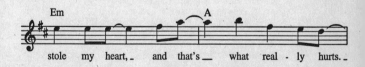

save you from being a - lone. You

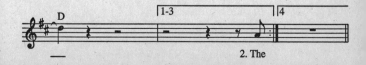

stole my heart, ___ and that's ___ what real - ly hurts. ___

___ 2. The

(Instrumental)

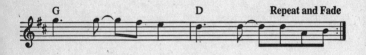

Repeat and Fade

Additional Lyrics

2. The morning sun, when it's in your face,
   Really shows your age.
   But that don't worry me none.
   In my eyes, you're everything.
   I laughed at all of your jokes.
   My love you didn't need to coax.
   Oh, Maggie, I couldn't have tried any more.
   You led me away from home
   Just to save you from being alone.
   You stole my soul, and that's a pain I can do without.

3. All I needed was a friend
   To lend a guiding hand.
   But you turned into a lover, and, mother, what a lover!
   You wore me out.
   All you did was wreck my bed,
   And, in the morning, kick me in the head.
   Oh, Maggie, I couldn't have tried any more.
   You led me away from home
   'Cause you didn't want to be alone.
   You stole my heart. I couldn't leave you if I tried.

4. I suppose I could collect my books
   And get on back to school.
   Or steal my daddy's cue
   And make a living out of playing pool.
   Or find myself a rock 'n' roll band
   That needs a helping hand.
   Oh, Maggie, I wish I'd never seen your face.
   You made a first-class fool out of me.
   But I'm as blind as a fool can be.
   You stole my heart, but I love you anyway.

MR. JONES

Words by ADAM DURITZ
Music by ADAM DURITZ and DAVID BRYSON

Bright Rock

I was down at the New Am - ster - dam star-ing at this yel - low-haired girl.__ Mis-ter Jones__ __ strikes up a con - ver - sa - tion with this black- - haired fla - men - co danc - er. You know, she__ __ danc - es while his fa - ther plays gui - tar. She's sud - den - ly beau - ti - ful. Well, we all__

___ want some - thing beau - ti - ful.

Man, I wish I was beau - ti - ful. So, come

dance this si - lence down___ through the morn - ing.

Sha - la - la - la - la - la - la - la, ___ yeah.

Uh huh, yeah.___

Cut up, Ma - ri - a!
will paint my pic - ture,

Show me some of them___ Span - ish danc - es.
paint my - self in blue and red and black and gray.

tell each oth-er fair - y tales____ and we
look in - to the fu - ture and we

stare at the beau-ti-ful wom-en. "She's look-
stare at the beau-ti-ful wom-en. "She's look-

ing at you. Ah, no, no, she's look-ing at me."__
ing at you. Oh, I don't think so. She's look-ing at me."__

__ Smil - ing in the bright_ lights,
__ Stand - ing in the spot - light,

com - ing through in ster - e - o. When
I bought my - self a gray gui - tar. When

ev - 'ry-bod - y loves____ you,__
ev - 'ry-bod - y loves____ me,__

you can nev-er be lone - ly.__ Well, I

I will nev-er be lone - ly.

I will nev-er be lone - ly.

Said, I'm nev-er gon-na be lone -

- ly. I want to be a li-

on. Yeah, ev-'ry-bod-

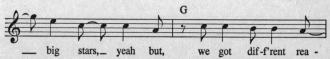

y wants to pass as cats. We all want to be big,

big stars, yeah but, we got dif-f'rent rea-

- sons for that. Be - lieve_ in me be - cause I

don't be - lieve_ in an - y - thing and I___

___ want to be some - one to___ be - lieve,

to be - lieve, to___ be - lieve, yeah.___

Mis - ter Jones and___ me
Mis - ter Jones and___ me

stum - bling through the bar - ri - o. Yeah, we
star - ing at the vid - e - o. When I

stare at the beau - ti - ful wom - en. "She's per -
look at the tel - e - vi - sion I want to

fect for you. Man, there's got to be___ some-bod-y for me."___
see me   star - ing___ right back at   me.___

___ I want to be Bob Dyl - an.   Mis - ter Jones___
___ We all want to be big stars,   but we don't___

___ wish - es he was some-one just a lit - tle more___ funk - y.
___ know why   and we don't   know how.   But

Where ev - 'ry - bod - y   loves___ you,   ah,   son,
when ev - 'ry - bod - y   loves___ me,   I'm going to be

that's just a - bout as funk - y as you___ can be.
just a - bout as hap - py as I___ can be.

Mis - ter   Jones   and___ me,

Freely

we're gon - na be big   stars...

MORE THAN WORDS

Words and Music by NUNO BETTENCOURT
and GARY CHERONE

Moderate Rock

Say-in', "I love you" is
Now that I've tried to

not the words I want to hear from you.
talk to you and make you un-der-stand.

It's not that I want you
All you have to do is

not to say. But if you on-ly knew
close your eyes and just reach out your hands.

how eas-y
and touch me,

it would be to show me how you feel,
hold me close, don't ev-er let me go.

121

123

NIGHT MOVES

Words and Music by
BOB SEGER

I was a lit - tle too tall, could - a used a few pounds. __ Tight pants, points, hard - ly re - nown. __ She was a black-haired __ beau - ty with big, dark eyes, _____ and points all her own, _ sit - tin' way up high, _ way up firm and high. _____ Out past the corn - fields, where the woods __ got heav - y,

out in the back seat of my Six - ty Chev-y,

work-in'. on mys-t'ries with-out an-y clues, ____

work-in' on our night moves, _

try'n' to make _ some front page, drive-in news. _

—— Work-in' on our night moves

in the sum-mer-time. ____

Mm, ____ in the sweet

sum-mer-time. ____

128

the won-der. ___

We felt the light-ning.   Yeah, ___

and we wait-ed on the thun-der,

wait-ed on the thun-der. _____

Freely

I a-woke last night to the

sound of thun-der.   How far off, I

sat and won-dered.   Start-ed hum-ming a song ___ from

nine-teen six-ty-two. ___

PINK HOUSES

Words and Music by
JOHN MELLENCAMP

- i - ca, for you and me!___ Ain't that A - mer-

- i - ca some - thin' to see,___

___ ba - by! Ain't that A - mer - i - ca, home of the free! _

___ Yeah, ___ lit - tle pink hous - es for

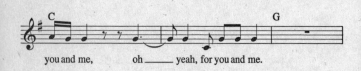

you and me, oh ___ yeah, for you and me.

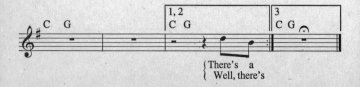

{ There's a
{ Well, there's

NORWEGIAN WOOD
(This Bird Has Flown)

**Words and Music by JOHN LENNON
and PAUL McCARTNEY**

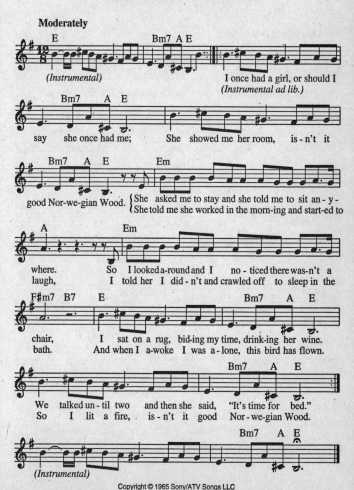

ONLY WANNA BE WITH YOU

Words and Music by DARIUS CARLOS RUCKER,
EVERETT DEAN FELBER, MARK WILLIAM BRYAN
and JAMES GEORGE SONEFELD

Moderately fast Rock

You and me,__ we come from dif-f'rent worlds.__

You like to laugh__ at me when I look__

__ at oth - er girls. __

Some - times you're cra - zy

and you won - der why __

I'm such a ba - by 'cause the Dol -

135

I won't dance,. you won't sing. _
"Said I shot a man _ named Gray," took his wife to It - a - ly.
Some-times you're cra-zy and you won - der why _

I just want to love _ you, but _ you want _
She in - her - its a mil - lion bucks and when she
I'm such a ba - by, yeah, _ the Dol -

_ to wear _ my ring. Well, there's noth-ing I _ can do, _
died it came _ to me. I can't help it if _ I'm luck-y."
- phins make _ me cry. Well, there's noth-ing I _ can do, _

I on - ly wan - na be with you. _
On - ly wan - na be with you. _
on - ly wan - na be with you. _

You can
Ain't
You can

call me ____ your ____ fool,
Bob - by ____ so ____ cool?
call me ____ your ____ fool,

on - ly wan - na be with you. _

only wan - na be with you. ___

Guitar solo - ad lib.

Solo ends Yeah, I'm

tan - gled up ___ in blue, ___

140

PATIENCE

**Words and Music by W. AXL ROSE,
SLASH, IZZY STRADLIN', DUFF McKAGAN
and STEVEN ADLER**

Moderately slow Rock Ballad

(Whistling)

1. Shed a tear 'cause I'm miss-in' _____ you. _____
2. I sit here on the _____ stairs _____ 'cause I'd

I'm still al-right _____ to smile. _____
rath-er be _____ a-lone. _____

Girl, I think a-bout _____ you ev-'ry day _____ now.
If I can't have you _____ right now _____ I'll wait, _____ dear.

Was a time when I was-n't sure, _____ but you
Some-times I get so _____ tense _____ but I

set my mind at ease. _____
can't speed up _____ the time. _____ But

There is no doubt _____ you're in _____ my heart _____
you know, love, there's one _____ more thing _____ to con-sid

We won't fake it,   ah,   I'll ne - ver break it

cause I can't   take it.

D.S.
(take 3rd ending) 3

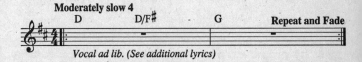

Moderately slow 4

D   D/F#   -   G   **Repeat and Fade**

Vocal ad lib. (See additional lyrics)

Additional Lyrics

(Vocal ad lib.)
Little patience, mm, yeah, mm, yeah.
Need a little patience, yeah.
Just a little patience.
I been walkin' the streets at night
Just tryin' to get it right.
Hard to see with so many around.
You know I don't like being stuck in the ground,
And the streets don't change, but baby the name.
I aint got time for the game 'cause I need you.
Yeah, yeah, but I need you, oo, I need you.
Whoa, I need you, oo, this time.

RUN AROUND

Words and Music by
JOHN POPPER

Brightly

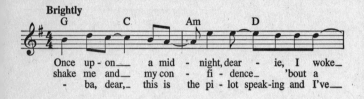

Once up-on__ a mid - night, dear - ie, I woke
shake me and__ my con - fi - dence__ 'bout a
\- ba, dear,__ this is the pi - lot speak-ing and I've__

__ with some-thing in my head.__ I
great man - y things,__ but I've been__
__ got some news for you.__ It seems my

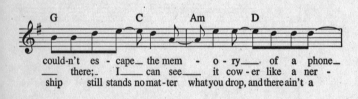

could-n't es - cape__ the mem - o - ry__ of a phone__
__ there; I__ can see__ it cow - er like a ner -
ship still stands no mat - ter what you drop, and there ain't a

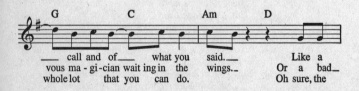

__ call and of__ what you said.__ Like a
vous ma - gi-cian wait ing in the wings.__ Or a bad__
whole lot that you can do. Oh sure, the

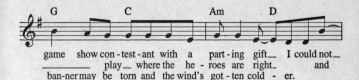

G   C   Am   D

game show con-test-ant with a part-ing gift. I could not_

_____ play_ where the he - roes are right_ and

ban-ner may be torn and the wind's got - ten cold - er.

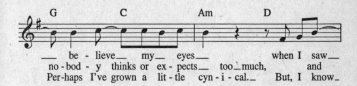

G   C   Am   D

_ be - lieve_ my eyes_ when I saw_

no - bod - y thinks or ex - pects_ too_much, and

Per-haps I've grown a lit - tle cyn - i - cal._ But, I know_

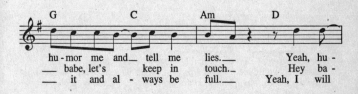

G   C   Am   D

through the voice of a trust - ed friend who needs to

Hol - ly-wood's call-ing for the mov-ie rights,_ sing-ing, "Hey_

_ no mat-ter what_ the wait - ress brings,_ I shall drink_

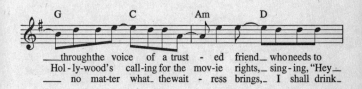

G   C   Am   D

hu - mor me and_ tell me lies._ Yeah, hu-

_ babe, let's keep in touch._ Hey ba-

_ it and al - ways be full._ Yeah, I will

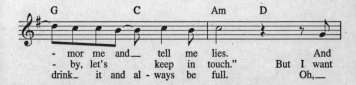

G   C   Am   D

\- mor me and_ tell me lies._ And

\- by, let's keep in touch." But I want

drink_ it and al - ways be full. Oh,_

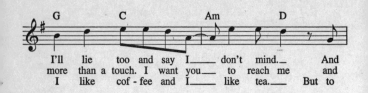

G   C   Am   D

I'll lie too and say I___ don't mind.___ And
more than a touch. I want you___ to reach me and
I like cof - fee and I___ like tea.___ But to

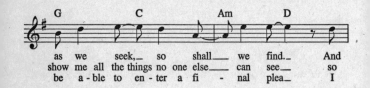

G   C   Am   D

as we seek,___ so shall___ we find.___ And
show me all the things no one else___ can see___ so
be a - ble to en - ter a fi - nal plea___ I

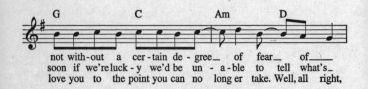

G   C   Am   D

when you're feel - ing o - pen I'll still___ be here,___ but
what___ you feel___ be - comes mine___ as well,___ and
still got___ this dream that you just___ can't shake.___ I

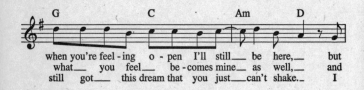

G   C   Am   D

not with - out a cer - tain de - gree___ of fear___ of ___
soon if we're luck - y we'd be un - a - ble to tell what's___
love you to the point you can no long er take. Well, all right,

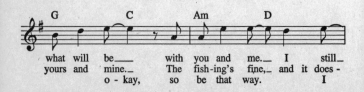

G   C   Am   D

what will be___ with you and me.___ I still
yours and mine.___ The fish - ing's fine, and it does -
o - kay, so be that way. I

148

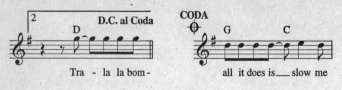

Tra - la la bom-   all it does is ___ slow me

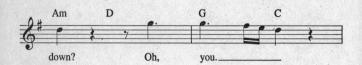

down?   Oh,   you. _____

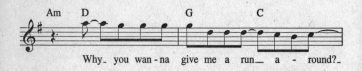

Why_ you wan - na give me a run__ a - round?_

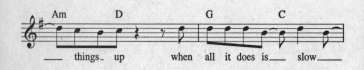

___ Is___ it a sure - fire way to speed_

___ things_ up   when all it does is___ slow___

Repeat and Fade

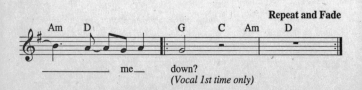

_____ me__   down?
(Vocal 1st time only)

SHOW ME THE WAY

Words and Music by
PETER FRAMPTON

SEVEN BRIDGES ROAD

Words and Music by
STEPHEN T. YOUNG

moon - light and moss
taste of time -

in the trees }
sweet - ened hon - ey }   down the

Sev - en Bridg -

To Coda

es Road.

Bright Country

Now, I have
I have

loved you
loved you

like a ba - by,
in a tame way and

like some lone -
I have loved

- some child.
you wild.

And
Some - times

there's a part

of me

155

SIGNS

Words and Music by
LES EMMERSON

Moderately slow

And the sign says, "Long - haired, freak - y peo - ple
sign says "Any - body caught tres - pass - ing
sign says, "Every - body wel - come, come

need not __ ap - ply." __ So I __
will be shot on sight." __ So I __
in and kneel down and pray." __ And then they

__ tucked my hair up un - der my hat and I
__ jumped the fence and yelled in the house, "Hey,
pass a - round the plate at the end of the hour, and I

went in to ask him why. __
what gives you the right __ to
did - n't have a penny to pay. __ So I

He said, "You look like a fine, __ out - stand - ing young
put up a fence to keep me out or to
get me a pen and pa - per, and I

man, __ I think you'll do." __ Uh, so I
keep moth - er na - ture in?" __ If
made up my own lit - tle sign. __ I said,

took off my hat and said, "Im - ag - ine that, huh,
God was here he'd tell it to your face,
"Thank you, Lord, for think - in' a - bout me. I'm a -

me a - work - ing for you." _ Oh. _____
"Man, you're some kind of sinner."
live and do - in' fine." _ Oh. _____

Signs, signs ev - 'ry - where a sign block -

- ing out the scen - er - y, break - ing my mind.

Do this don't _ do _ that. Can't you read _ the sign? _

1
And the

2
Oh. Uh, say now, mis - ter, can't _ you read? You

158

got to have a shirt and tie___ to get a seat.___

You can't watch, no,___ you___ can't___ eat.

You ain't sup-posed to be here. _____ And the

sign said, "You got to have a mem - ber - ship

card to get in - side." Ooh!

D.S. al Coda

And the

CODA

Signs,_ signs ev - 'ry-where a sign block-

- ing out the scen - er - y, break - ing my mind.

Do this don't _ do _ that. Can't you read _ the sign? _____

SWEET TALKIN' WOMAN

Words and Music by
JEFF LYNNE

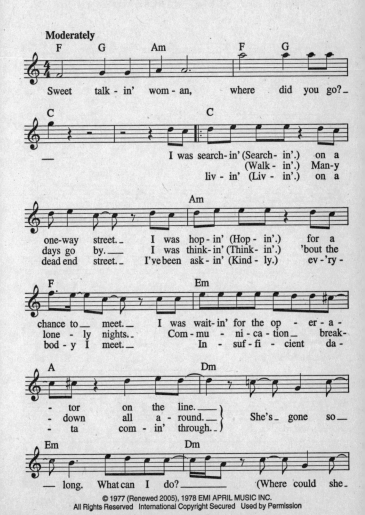

Moderately

Sweet talk-in' wom-an, where did you go?

I was search-in' (Search- in'.) on a
(Walk- in'.) Man-y
liv-in' (Liv- in'.) on a

one-way street. I was hop-in' (Hop- in'.) for a
days go by. I was think-in' (Think- in'.) 'bout the
dead end street. I've been ask-in' (Kind- ly.) ev-'ry-

chance to meet. I was wait-in' for the op- er-a-
lone-ly nights. Com-mu- ni-ca-tion break-
bod-y I meet. In- suf-fi- cient da-

- tor on the line. }
- down all a- round. } She's gone so
- ta com- in' through. }

— long. What can I do? (Where could she

SILENT LUCIDITY

Words and Music by
CHRIS DeGARMO

*1st time vocal is sung one octave lower than written

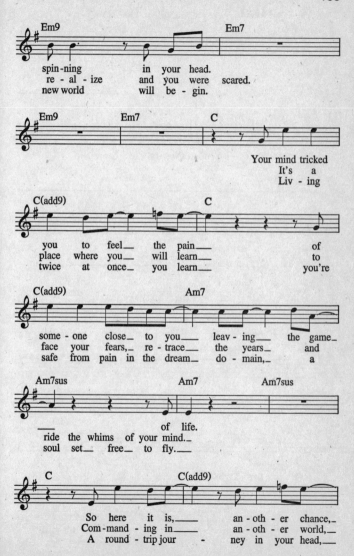

SOAK UP THE SUN

Words and Music by JEFF TROTT
and SHERYL CROW

167

CODA

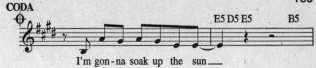

I'm gon-na soak up the sun

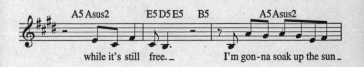

while it's still free. I'm gon-na soak up the sun

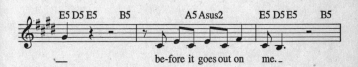

be-fore it goes out on me.

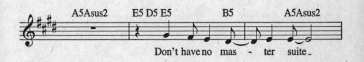

Don't have no mas - ter suite

but I'm still the king of me.

You have a fan - cy ride but ba - by,

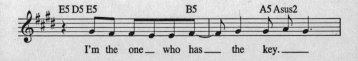

I'm the one who has the key.

Ev - 'ry time I turn a - round I'm

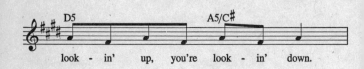

look - in' up, you're look - in' down.

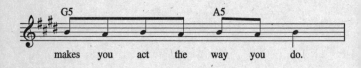

May - be some - thing's wrong with you that

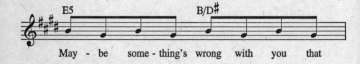

makes you act the way you do.

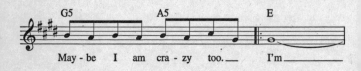

May - be I am cra - zy too.___ I'm___

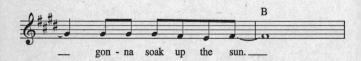

___ gon - na soak up the sun. ___

I'm gon - na tell ev - 'ry - one ___ to

171

SOMEBODY TO LOVE

Words and Music by
DARBY SLICK

174

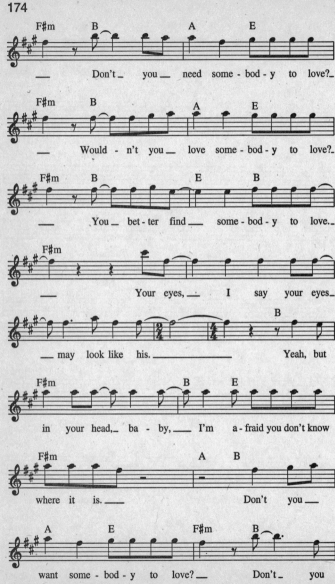

THE SPACE BETWEEN

Words and Music by
DAVID J. MATTHEWS and GLEN BALLARD

Moderately

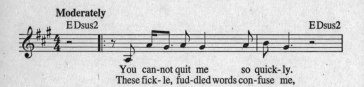

You can-not quit me   so quick-ly.
These fick-le, fud-dled words con-fuse me,

Is no hope in you___ for me.___
like will it rain to - day?

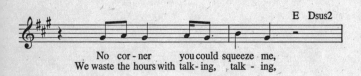

No cor - ner   you could squeeze me,
We waste the hours with talk-ing, talk - ing,

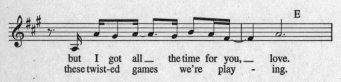

but I got all___ the time for you,___ love.
these twist-ed games we're play - ing.

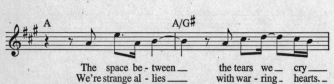

The space be - tween___ the tears we___ cry___
We're strange al - lies___ with war - ring hearts.___

is the laugh - ter keeps _ us com-ing back _ for more. _
What a wild - eyed _ beast you _ be. _

The space be - tween _ the wick-ed _ lies _

_ we tell _ and hope _ to keep us safe from the pain. _

1
But will I hold you a - gain?

2
But will I hold you a - gain? _

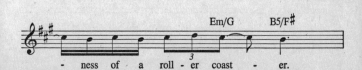

will I hold.... _ Look at us spin-ning out in the mad -

- ness of a roll - er coast - er.

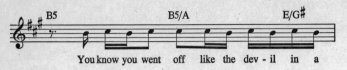

You know you went off like the dev-il in a

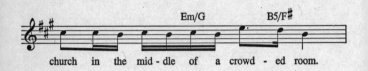

church in the mid-dle of a crowd-ed room.

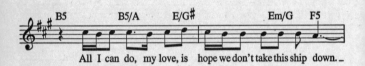

All I can do, my love, is hope we don't take this ship down.

The space be-tween __ where you __ smile __ and

hide __ is where you'll find __ me if I __ get to go. __

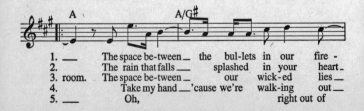

1. __ The space be-tween __ the bul-lets in our fire-
2. The rain that falls __ splashed in your heart __
3. room. The space be-tween __ our wick-ed lies __
4. Take my hand __ 'cause we're walk-ing out __
5. __ Oh, right out of

Dmaj9/F#   E/G#   **Play 5 times**

- fight   is   where   I'll be   hid-ing, wait-ing   for you.
—   ran   like   sad-ness   down the   win-dow   into your
—   is where   we   hope   to   keep   safe from pain.
—   of   here.
here.   Love   is   all   we need   dear.

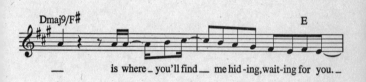

A   A

The space be-tween   what's wrong and right

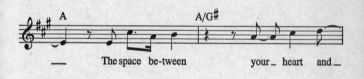

Dmaj9/F#   E

is where you'll find   me hid-ing, wait-ing for you.

A   A/G#

The space be-tween   your heart   and

Dmaj9/F#   E/G#

mine   is the   space   we'll fill with time.

A   A/G#   Dmaj9/F#   E/G#

The space be - tween...

SPACE ODDITY

Words and Music by
DAVID BOWIE

Slowly

Ground Con-trol _ to Ma - jor Tom. _

Ground Con-trol _ to Ma - jor Tom. _

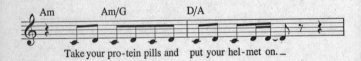

Take your pro-tein pills and put your hel-met on. _

Ground Con-trol _ to Ma - jor Tom. _

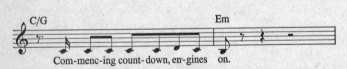

Com-menc-ing count-down, en-gines on.

Check ig - ni-tion and may God's love be with you.

N.C.

(Instrumental)

C/G

This is Ground Con-trol___ to Ma - jor Tom,___
This is Ma - jor Tom___ to Ground___ Con - trol,___

E7   F

___ you've real - ly made the grade. _____ And the
___ I'm step-ping though the door. _____ And I'm

Fm   C/G   F

pa - pers want to know whose shirts you wear.___ Now it's
float-ing in a most pe - cu - liar way.___ And the

1
Fm   C/G   F

time to leave the cap-sule if you dare. ___

2
Fm   C/G   F

stars look ver-y dif-fer-ent to - day. _____ For

Fmaj7/C   Em7

here   am I { sit - ting in a } tin can, ___
                  { float-ing 'round my }

far _____ a - bove_ the { world _____ / moon. _____ }

Plan-et Earth is blue, and there's noth-ing I can

do.   *(Instrumental)*

To Coda

Though I'm past one hun - dred thou - sand miles, _

_____ I'm feel-ing ver - y still. _____   And I

Guitar solo ad lib.

SUITE: JUDY BLUE EYES

Words and Music by
STEPHEN STILLS

Moderately fast

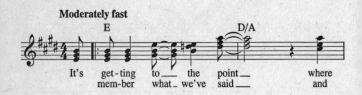

It's get-ting to the point where
mem-ber what we've said and

I'm no fun an-y-more.
done and felt a-bout each oth - er.

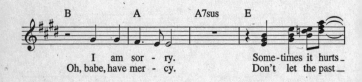

I am sor - ry. Some-times it hurts
Oh, babe, have mer - cy. Don't let the past

so bad - ly I must cry out loud.
re - mind us of what we are not now.

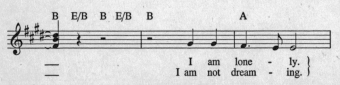

I am lone - ly. }
I am not dream - ing. }

I've ___ got an an - swer. ___
Will ___ you come see ___ me ___

I'm ___ go - ing ___ to fly a - way. ___
Thurs - days ___ and Sat - ur - days? ___

What have I got to lose? ___

1
E5

(Instrumental)

2
E5

(Instrumental)   *Half-time feel ends*   Chest - nut - brown ___ ca - nar-
Voic - es   of ___ the an -
Lac - y,   lilt - ing lyr-

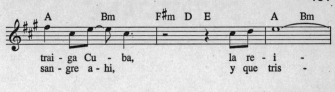

trai - ga Cu - ba,   la re - i -
san - gre a - hi,   y que tris -

-     na de la Mar - Car - i - be.
-     te que no

Cie - lo pue - do va - ya.

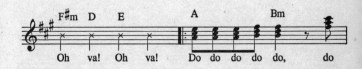

Oh va! Oh va!   Do do do do do,   do

do   do do do do,   do do do do do,   do

do   do do,   do   do do.

SWEET JANE

Words and Music by
LOU REED

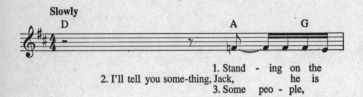

1. Stand - ing on the
2. I'll tell you some-thing, Jack,   he is

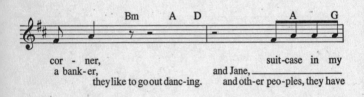

cor - ner,   suit-case in my
a bank- er,
      they like to go out danc-ing.   and oth-er peo-ples, they have

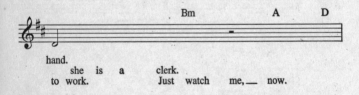

hand.
      she is a   clerk.
to work.   Just watch me, __ now.

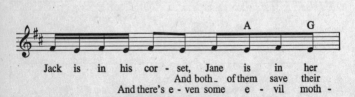

Jack is in his cor - set, Jane is in her
And both _ of them save their
And there's e - ven some e - vil moth -

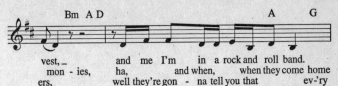

Bm A D   A   G

vest, _____ and me I'm in a rock and roll band.
mon - ies, ha, and when, when they come home
ers, well they're gon - na tell you that ev-'ry

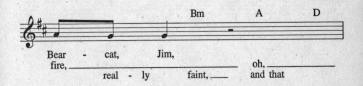

Bm   A   D   A 3 G

Huh. Rid-in' in a Stutz
from work. Ooh, sit - tin' down by the
thing is just dirt. Y'know that wom - en nev-er

Bm   A   D

Bear - cat, Jim,
fire, _____ oh, _____
real - ly faint, ___ and that

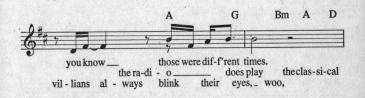

A   G   Bm A D

you know ___ those were dif-f'rent times.
the ra-di - o _____ does play the clas-si-cal
vil - lians al - ways blink their eyes, _ woo,

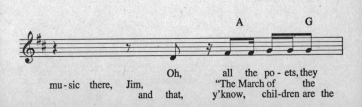

A   G

Oh, all the po - ets, they
mu - sic there, Jim, "The March of the
and that, y'know, chil - dren are the

stud - ied rules   of   verse, ___   and   those
Wood - en   Sol - diers."   All you pro - test
on - ly   ones   who   blush, ___

lad - ies, ___   they   rolled   their   eyes.
kids,   and   that   you can hear Jack
    life   is   just

3rd time: To Coda ⊕

say, ___   get read - y ah. }   Sweet   Jane, ___
to   die. ___

_____   whoa. ___   Sweet   Jane, ___

2nd time: D.C. al Coda

___   oh,   oh. ___   Sweet   Jane. ___

CODA ⊕

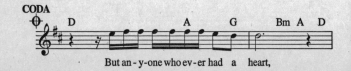

But an - y-one who ev - er had a   heart,

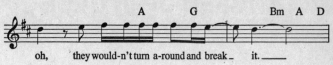

oh, they would-n't turn a-round and break it.

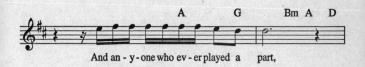

And an - y - one who ev - er played a part,

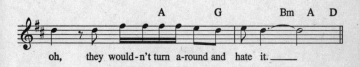

oh, they would-n't turn a-round and hate it.

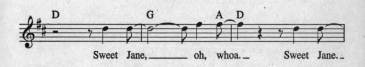

Sweet Jane, oh, whoa. Sweet Jane.

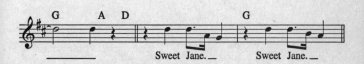

Sweet Jane. Sweet Jane.

Repeat and Fade

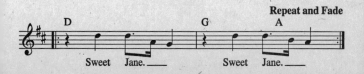

Sweet Jane. Sweet Jane.

TANGLED UP IN BLUE

Words and Music by
BOB DYLAN

Moderately

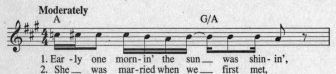

1. Ear-ly one morn-in' the sun was shin-in',
2. She was mar-ried when we first met,
3. I had a job in the great North woods,

4.-7. *(See additional lyrics)*

8. *Instrumental*

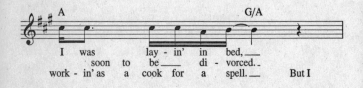

I was lay-in' in bed,
soon to be di-vorced.
work-in' as a cook for a spell. But I

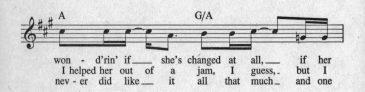

won - d'rin' if she's changed at all, if her
I helped her out of a jam, I guess, but I
nev - er did like it all that much and one

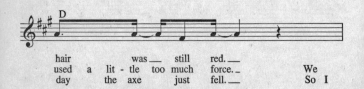

hair was still red.
used a lit-tle too much force. We
day the axe just fell. So I

A   **G/A**

Her folks, they said our lives to - geth - er
drove that car as far as we could, — a -
drift - ed down to New Or - leans. — I was

A   **G/A**

sure was gon - na be rough. — They
ban - doned it out west. —
luck - y to be em - ployed, —

A   **G**

nev - er did like Ma-ma's home made dress, — Pa - pa's
Split up — on the docks that night, — both a -
work-in' for a while on a fish - in' boat — right —

D

bank book was — n't big e - nough. And
gree - ing it — was best. — As
out - side of — Del - a - croix. —

E   **F#m**

I was stand - in' on the side of the road, — rain —
she turned a - round — to look at — me, — as
But all the while, — I — was — a - lone, — the

A   **D**

— fall - in' on my shoes, —
I was — walk - in' a - way,
past was — close be - hind. —

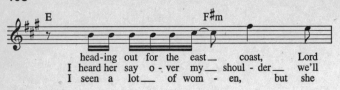

head-ing out for the east __ coast, Lord
I heard her say o - ver my __ shoul - der __ we'll
I seen a lot __ of wom - en, but she

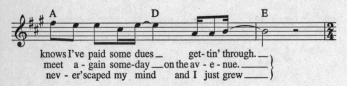

knows I've paid some dues __ get-tin' through. __
meet a - gain some-day __ on the av - e - nue. _____
nev - er'scaped my mind and I just grew _____

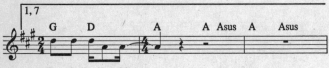

Tan-gled up in blue. __
tan-gled up in blue. __

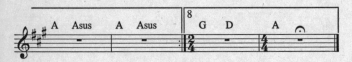

Additional Lyrics

4. She was working in a topless place
And I stopped in for a beer.
I just kept looking at the side of her face
In the spotlight so clear.
And later on when the crowd thinned out
I was just about to do the same.
She was standing there in back of my chair,
Said to me, "Don't I know your name?"
I muttered something underneath my breath.
She studied the lines on my face.
I must admit I felt a little uneasy
When she bent down to tie the laces of my shoe,
Tangled up in blue.

5. She lit a burner on the stove
   And offered me a pipe.
   "I thought you'd never say hello," she said.
   "You look like the silent type."
   Then she opened up a book of poems
   And handed it to me,
   Written by an Italian poet
   From the thirteenth century.
   And every one of them words rang true
   And glowed like burning coal,
   Pourin' off of every page
   Like it was written in my soul,
   From me to you,
   Tangled up in blue.

6. I lived with them on Montague Street
   In a basement down the stairs.
   There was music in the cafes at night
   And revolution in the air.
   Then he started in the dealing in slaves
   And something inside of him died.
   She had to sell everything she owned
   And froze up inside.
   And when finally the bottom finally fell out
   I became withdrawn.
   The only thing I knew how to do
   Was to keep on keeping on,
   Like a bird that flew
   Tangled up in blue.

7. So now I'm going back again.
   I got to get to her somehow.
   All the people we used to know,
   They're an illusion to me now.
   Some are mathematicians,
   Some are carpenter's wives.
   Don't know how it all got started,
   I don't know what they do with their lives.
   But me, I'm still on the road
   Headin' for another joint.
   We always did feel the same,
   We just saw it from a different point of view,
   Tangled up in blue.

TEACH YOUR CHILDREN

Words and Music by
GRAHAM NASH

201

202

TEARS IN HEAVEN

Words and Music by ERIC CLAPTON
and WILL JENNINGS

THICK AS A BRICK

Words and Music by
IAN ANDERSON

to be thick

as a brick.

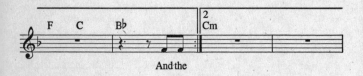

And the

And the love that I

feel   is

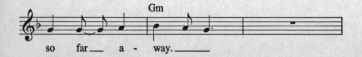

so far   a - way.

209

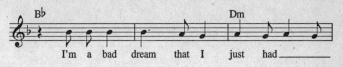

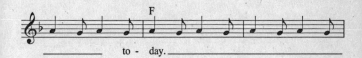

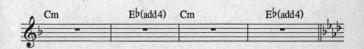

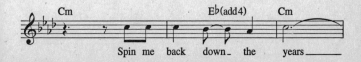

TIME FOR ME TO FLY

Words and Music by
KEVIN CRONIN

Moderately slow, in 2

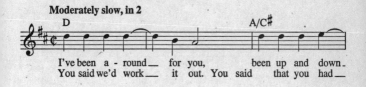

I've been a - round__ for you, been up and down__
You said we'd work__ it out. You said that you had__

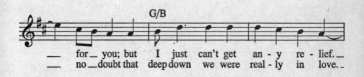

__ for you; but I just can't get an - y re - lief.__
__ no__ doubt that deep down we were real - ly in love.__

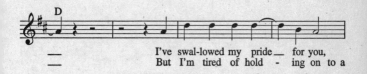

__ I've swal-lowed my pride__ for you,
__ But I'm tired of hold - ing on to a

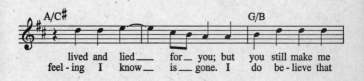

lived and lied__ for you; but you still make me
feel - ing I know__ is__ gone. I do be - lieve that

feel like a thief.__ You got me
I've had e - nough.__ I've had e -

212

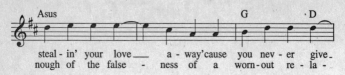

steal - in' your love ___ a - way 'cause you nev - er give ___
nough of the false - ness of a worn - out re - la -

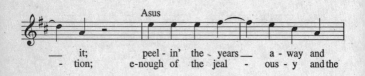

___ it; peel - in' the years ___ a - way and
- tion; e-nough of the jeal - ous - y and the

we can't re - live ___ it. }
in - tol - er - a - tion. } I make you laugh, ___

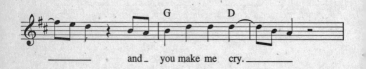

and ___ you make me cry. ___

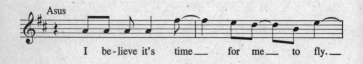

I be - lieve it's time ___ for me ___ to fly. ___

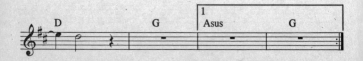

Time for me to fly.

I've got to set my - self free. Time for me to fly.

That's just how it's got to be.

I know it hurts to say good -

bye, but it's time for me to fly.

It's

time for me to fly.

3 AM

Lyrics by ROB THOMAS
Music by ROB THOMAS, BRIAN YALE,
JOHN LESLIE GOFF and JOHN JOSEPH STANLEY

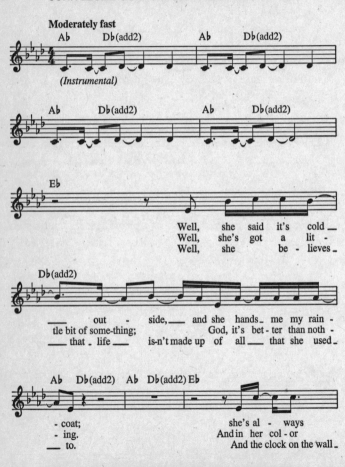

Moderately fast

(Instrumental)

Well, she said it's cold ___ ___ out - side, ___ and she hands ___ me my rain - coat;
Well, she's got a lit - tle bit of some-thing; God, it's bet - ter than noth - ing. she's al - ways And in her col - or
Well, she be - lieves ___ that life ___ is-n't made up of all ___ that she used ___ to. And the clock on the wall ___

TO BE WITH YOU

Words and Music by ERIC MARTIN
and DAVID GRAHAME

Moderately

C#m · · · · · · E

Hold on, ___ lit - tle girl.
Build up ___ your con - fi - dence so

A(add9) · · · · · · E

Show me what ___ he's done ___ to you.
you can be ___ on top ___ for once.

C#m · · · · · · E

Stand up, ___ lit - tle girl. A
Wake up. ___ Who cares a - bout

A(add9) · · · · · · E

bro - ken heart ___ can't be ___ that bad. ___ When
lit - tle boys ___ that talk ___ too much? ___ I've

A(add9) · · · · · · E

it's through, ___ it's through. ___
seen it all go down. ___ The

A(add9) · · · · · · E

Fate will twist ___ the both ___ of you. ___ So
game of love ___ was all ___ rained out. ___ So

219

come on, ba - by, come on o - ver.
come on, ba - by, come on o - ver.

Let me be ___ the one ___ to show ___ you.)
Let me be ___ the one ___ to hold ___ you.)

I'm the one who wants to be with you. ___

Deep in - side I hope you'll feel ___ it, too. ___

Wait - ed on a line of greens and blues ___

just to be the next to be ___ with you. ___

be ___ with you. ___ Why be a - lone ___ when we can

be to - geth - er, ba - by?

You can make my life worth-while.

I can make you start to smile.

(Instrumental)

When

it's through, it's through. And

fate will twist the both of you. So

come on, ba-by, come on o-ver.

Let me be the one to show you.

222

TORN

Words and Music by PHIL THORNALLEY,
SCOTT CUTLER and ANNE PREVIN

Moderate Rock

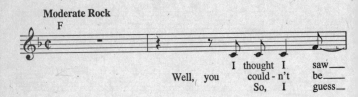

I thought I saw __
Well, you could - n't be __
So, I guess __

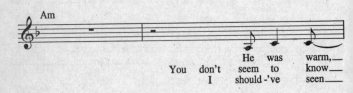

__ a man __ brought __ to life.
__ that man __ I __ a - dored. __
__ the for - tune tell - er's right. __

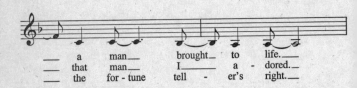

He was warm,
You don't seem to know __
I should -'ve seen

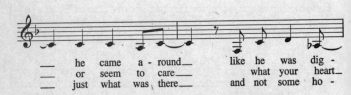

__ he came a - round __ like he was dig -
__ or seem to care __ what your heart
__ just what was there __ and not some ho -

225

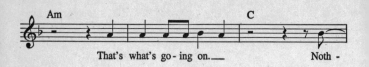

That's what's go-ing on.___ Noth-

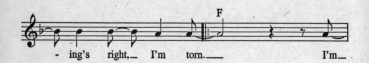

-ing's right, I'm torn.___ I'm___

___ all out of faith,___ this___ is how___ I feel.___

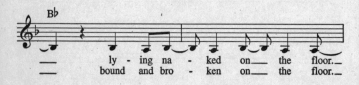

___ I'm cold and { I___ am shamed,___
{ I'm___ a - shamed,___

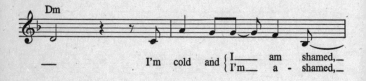

___ ly - ing na - ked on___ the floor.___
___ bound and bro - ken on___ the floor.___

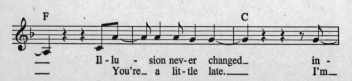

___ Il - lu - sion nev-er changed___ in-le-
___ You're___ a lit - tle late.___ I'm___

WANTED DEAD OR ALIVE

Words and Music by JON BON JOVI
and RICHIE SAMBORA

Moderately slow

It's all the same, on - ly the names will change, _____ The
times I sleep, _ some-times it's not _ for days. _____
Instrumental solo

ev - 'ry day, _ it seems we're wast-ing a - way. _ An-
peo - ple I meet al - ways go their sep - 'rate ways. Some

oth - er place, _ where the fac - es are _ so cold. I'd
times you tell _ the day _ by the bot - tle that you drink. And

drive all night, _____ just to get back home. _ I'm a
times when you're a - lone, _ all you do is think. I'm a
Solo ends

cow - boy, on a steel _ horse. I ride. I'm

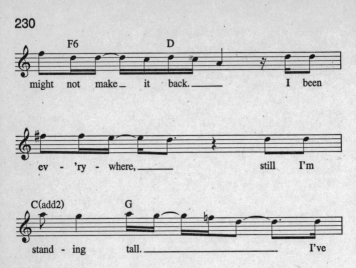

might not make it back. _____ I been

ev - 'ry - where, _____ still I'm

stand - ing tall. _____ I've

seen a mil - lion fac - es _____ and I've

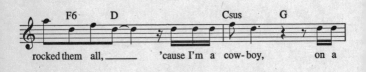

rocked them all, _____ 'cause I'm a cow-boy, on a

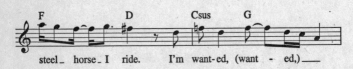

steel _ horse _ I ride. I'm want-ed, (want - ed,) _____

dead or a - live. _ 'Cause I'm a cow-boy. I got the

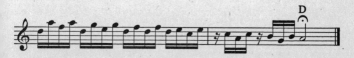

WHAT I GOT

Words and Music by BRAD NOWELL,
ERIC WILSON, FLOYD GAUGH and LINDON ROBERTS

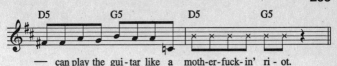

— can play the gui - tar like a moth-er-fuck-in' ri - ot.

Well, life

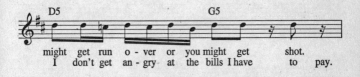

is (too short) so love_ the one you got 'cause you
Why, I don't cry when my dog runs_ a - way.

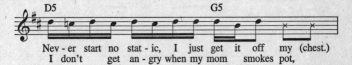

might get run o - ver or you might get shot.
I don't get an - gry at the bills I have to pay.

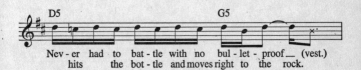

Nev - er start no stat - ic, I just get it off my (chest.)
I don't get an - gry when my mom smokes pot,

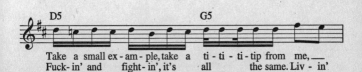

Nev - er had to bat - tle with no bul - let - proof_ (vest.)
hits the bot - tle and moves right to the rock.

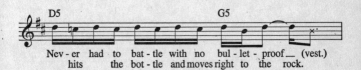

Take a small ex - am - ple, take a ti - ti - ti - tip from me, _
Fuck - in' and fight - in', it's all the same. Liv - in'

235

D5 G5 D5 G5
Lov - in' is what I got. and re-mem-ber that.
D5 G5 D5 G7
Lov - in' is what I got. I said re-mem-ber that.
D.S. al Coda
D5 G5 D G7
Lov - in' is what I got. I got, I got, I got.
CODA
D5 D5 C5 G5 D5 C5 G5
to me
D5 C5 G5 D5 C5 G5 D5
'Cause
D5 C5 G5 D5 C5 G5
lov - in' is what I got. I said re-mem-ber that. Lov-
D5 C5 G5 D5 C5 G5
- in' is what I got. and re-mem-ber that Lov-
D5 C5 G5 D5 C5 G5
- in' is what I got. I said re-mem-ber that Lov-
D5 C5 G5 D5
- in' is what I got. I got, I got, I got.

WHEN THE CHILDREN CRY

Words and Music by MIKE TRAMP
and VITO BRATTA

Smoothly, with motion

G · D/F# · Em

Lit-tle child, ___   dry your cry-
Lit-tle child, ___   you must
Guitar solo ad lib.

Bm · C · G

- in' eyes. ___   How can I ___ ex-plain ___ the
show the way ___   to a bet-ter day ___ for

Em · D · G

fear you feel ___ in-side? ___   'Cause you were born ___
all the young.   'Cause you were born ___

D/F# · Em · Bm

___ in-to this e-vil world
___ for the world to see

C · G

where man is kill-ing man ___ and
that we all can live ___ with

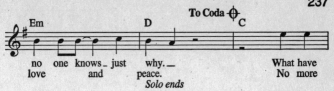

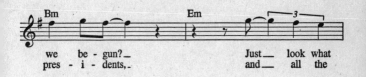

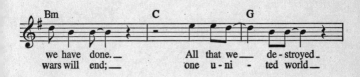

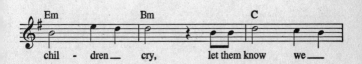

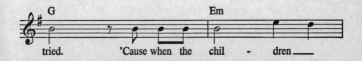

238

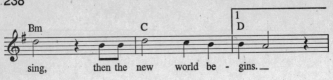

sing, then the new world be - gins. _

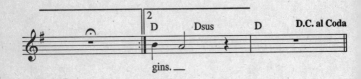

D.C. al Coda

gins. _

CODA

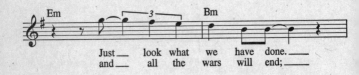

What have we be - gun? _
No more pres - i - dents, _

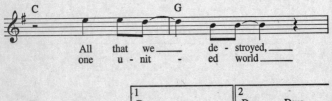

Just _ look what we have done. _
and _ all the wars will end; _

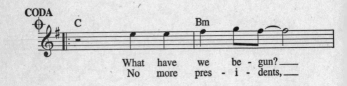

All that we _ de - stroyed, _
one u - nit - ed world _

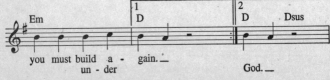

you must build a - gain. _
un - der God. _

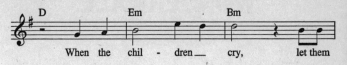

When the chil - dren___ cry, let them

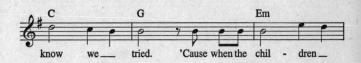

know we___ tried. 'Cause when the chil - dren___

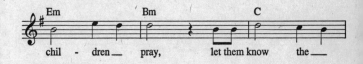

fight, let them know it ain't right.___ When the

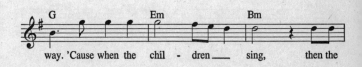

chil - dren___ pray, let them know the___

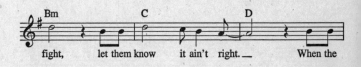

way. 'Cause when the chil - dren___ sing, then the

new world be - gins.___

WONDERWALL

Words and Music by
NOEL GALLAGHER

Moderately

To - day   is   gon - na   be   the   day   that they're

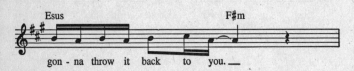

gon - na throw   it   back   to   you. __

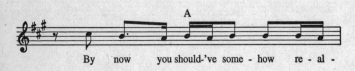

By   now   you should-'ve some - how   re - al -

ized   what   you   got - ta   do. __

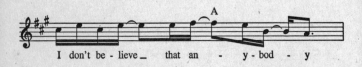

I   don't be - lieve __   that   an - y - bod - y

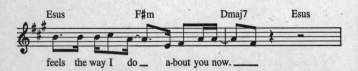

feels   the   way   I   do __   a-bout you now. __

THE WORLD I KNOW

Words and Music by ED ROLAND
and ROSS BRIAN CHILDRESS

Has our con-science shown?
Has all kind-ness gone?
Are we lis-ten-ing?
Have we eyes to see?

Has the
Hope still
Hymns of
Love is

1,3 sweet breeze blown?
of-fer-ing.

2,4 lin-gers on.
gath-er-ing.

(1., D.S.) I drink my-self of new-found pit-y
All the words that I've been read-ing

sit-ting a-lone in New York Cit-y, and I don't know why.
have now start-ed the act of bleed-ing in-to one.

1.
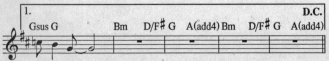

245

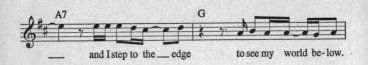

_____ and I step to the _____ edge   to see my   world be-low.

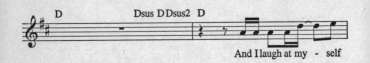

And I laugh at my - self

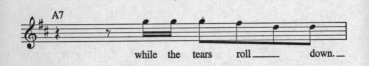

while   the   tears   roll _____   down. _____

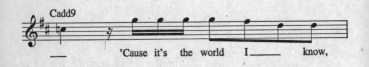

_____   'Cause it's   the   world   I _____   know,

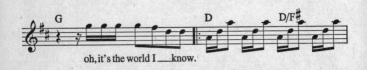

oh, it's the world I _____ know.

YOU'VE GOT A FRIEND

Words and Music by
CAROLE KING

When you're down _____ and trou-
a - bove

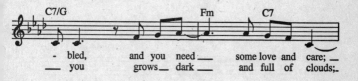

- bled, and you need _____ some love and care;
_____ you grows _____ dark _____ and full of clouds; _____

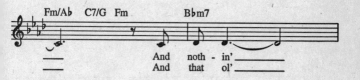

And noth - in' _____
And that ol' _____

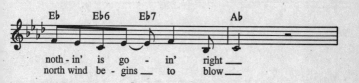

noth - in' is go - in' right _____
north wind be - gins _____ to blow _____

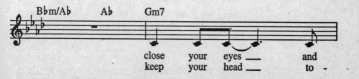

close your eyes _____ and
keep your head _____ to -

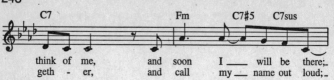

think of me, and soon I __ will be there;
geth - er, and call my __ name out loud; __

__ To bright - en up __ e - me
__ Soon you'll hear __ me __

- ven your dark - est night. __
__ knock - in' at __ your door. __

You just call __ out my __ name, __

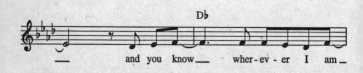

__ and you know __ wher - ev - er I am __

__ I'll come run - nin' __

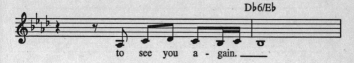

Db6/Eb

to see you a - gain. ____

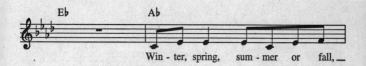

Eb   Ab

Win - ter, spring, sum - mer or fall, ___

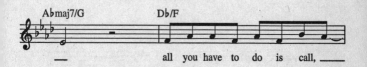

Abmaj7/G   Db/F

___ all you have to do is call, ____

Ab6/Eb   Ab7/Eb   **To Coda** ⊕

_____ and I'll be ____

1.
Db   Cm7   Bbm7 Db6/Eb

___ there. _____ You've Got A Friend..

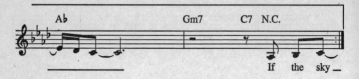

If the sky _

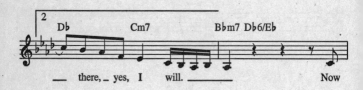

_ there, _ yes, I will. _____ Now

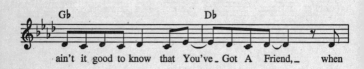

ain't it good to know that You've _ Got A Friend, _ when

peo - ple can be _ so cold. _ They'll hurt _

_ you, yes, and de - sert _ you, and

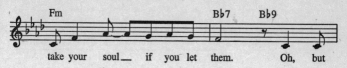

take your soul___ if you let them. Oh, but

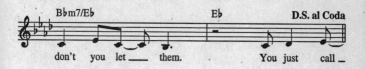

don't you let ___ them. You just call ___

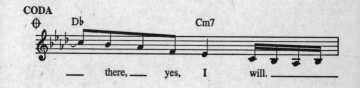

CODA

___ there, ___ yes, I will. _____

___ You've Got A Friend. _____ You've Got A

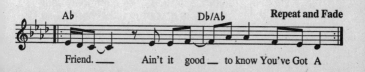

Friend. ___ Ain't it good ___ to know You've Got A

GUITAR CHORD FRAMES

	C	Cm	C+	C6	Cm6
C					

	C#	C#m	C#+	C#6	C#m6
C#/Db					

	D	Dm	D+	D6	Dm6
D					

	Eb	Ebm	Eb+	Eb6	Ebm6
Eb/D#					

	E	Em	E+	E6	Em6
E					

	F	Fm	F+	F6	Fm6
F					

This guitar chord reference includes 120 commonly used chords. For a more complete guide to guitar chords, see "THE PAPERBACK CHORD BOOK" (HL00702009).

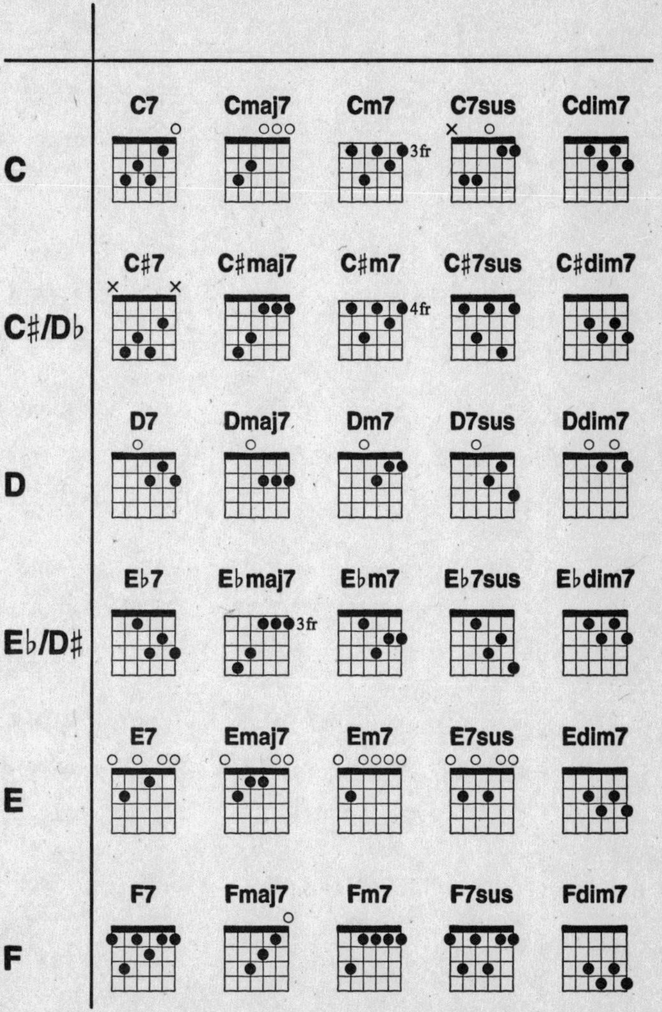
C
C7
Cmaj7
Cm7
3fr
C7sus
Cdim7
C♯/D♭
C♯7
C♯maj7
C♯m7
4fr
C♯7sus
C♯dim7
D
D7
Dmaj7
Dm7
D7sus
Ddim7
E♭/D♯
E♭7
E♭maj7
3fr
E♭m7
E♭7sus
E♭dim7
E
E7
Emaj7
Em7
E7sus
Edim7
F
F7
Fmaj7
Fm7
F7sus
Fdim7

254

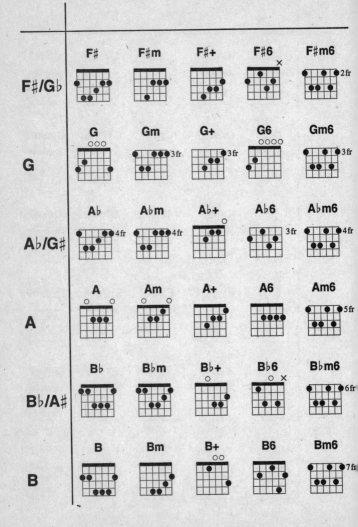

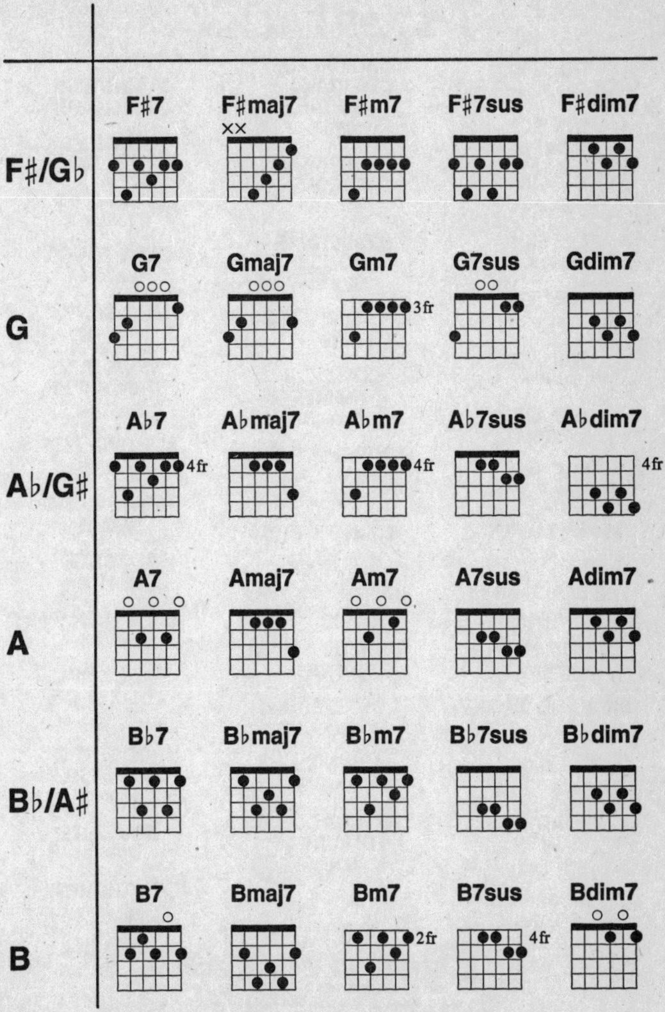
F♯/G♭
F♯7
F♯maj7
F♯m7
F♯7sus
F♯dim7
G
G7
Gmaj7
Gm7
3fr
G7sus
Gdim7
A♭/G♯
A♭7
4fr
A♭maj7
A♭m7
4fr
A♭7sus
A♭dim7
4fr
A
A7
Amaj7
Am7
A7sus
Adim7
B♭/A♯
B♭7
B♭maj7
B♭m7
B♭7sus
B♭dim7
B
B7
Bmaj7
Bm7
2fr
B7sus
4fr
Bdim7